MW01121517

Starting SMALL :
Thinking BIG

Practical Strategies
For School Success

Starting SMALL:
Thinking BIG

Practical Strategies
For School Success

Chris Alexiou

Mosaic Press
Oakville, ON - Buffalo, N.Y.

Canadian Cataloguing in Publication Data

Alexiou, Chris, 1954-
    Starting small, thinking big : pracitical strategies for school success

ISBN 0-88962-579-4

1. Home and school.   2. Education - Parent participation.
3. Academic achievement.   I. Title.

LC223.A54 1994   694'.68   C94-932835-9

Published by MOSAIC PRESS, P.O. Box 1032, Oakville, Ontario, L6J 5E9, Canada. Offices and warehouse at 1252 Speers Road, Units #1&2, Oakville, Ontario, L6L 5N9, Canada and Mosaic Press, 85 River Rock Drive, Suite 202, Buffalo, N.Y., 14207, USA.

Mosaic Press acknowledges the assistance of the Canada Council, the Ontario Arts Council, the Ontario Ministry of Culture, Tourism and Recreation and the Dept. of Communications, Government of Canada, for their support of our publishing programme.

Cover and book design by Susan Parker
Printed and bound in Canada
ISBN 0-88962-579-4

In Canada:
    MOSAIC PRESS, 1252 Speers Road, Units #1&2, Oakville, Ontario, L6L 5N9, Canada. P.O. Box 1032, Oakville, Ontario, L6J 5E9
In the United States:
    Mosaic Press, 85 River Rock Drive, Suite 202, Buffalo, N.Y., 14207

This book is dedicated to
Lucy, Michael, Christina and Alexandra

Contents

Starting SMALL : Thinking BIG

Our Children

All of us want our children to succeed in all their endeavours. As they grow we want them to be accepted and well liked by their peers. We want their hurtful experiences to be few. Ideally, we would like our children to be strong, talented and self-assured, able to deal effectively with all situations that arise. Often, parents fear that these positive characteristics will be lost because of the influences of present day society: violence in the media, drugs, negative peer influences, family breakdown and low achievement in school. We want our children to have more opportunities than we had. Above all, we want them to accomplish all the goals they set for themselves and achieve a large measure of success and happiness.

Life is filled with adversity. Succeeding in adverse situations develops perseverance and a stronger character. Children should have the benefit of our love, knowledge and experience but also the opportunity to experience success and failure for themselves in order to appreciate and learn from the experience. Our role as parents, and educators, should be to prepare them with the necessary knowledge, skills and attitudes to achieve their goals and deal effectively with adverse situations they may encounter.

In order to achieve their goals children need as many doors open to them as possible, so they can make their own choices as they grow. Although predicting future success is difficult, there are many specific things parents can do to enhance their children's learning and, consequently, leave open all the doors needed for making future choices.

This book will provide parents and adults who work with children with specific and practical suggestions that, if followed consistently, should enhance learning and future school success.

Actions Speak Louder than Words

The French philosopher Rousseau described the newborn child as a "blank slate". He believed that a child's personal characteristics are not predetermined but develop based on the environment in which the child is raised. This theory has been supported and refuted many times during the last two hundred years. It is probably reasonable to assume that a child's development is affected to some degree by both genetic characteristics passed on by parents and the environment in which the child grows. If we consider genetics as something that is beyond our control, even today, the environment in which we raise our children and prepare them for future success becomes very important.

When we see children with their parents we often hear the remark that one child has the "mother's eyes" and the other the "father's chin". In most cases, children are smaller versions of their parents. The physical resemblance is definitely evident and other characteristics like sense of humour, disposition, anxiety, approach to situations and even use of certain words or phrases when speaking, are often very similar to either parent. The old adage holds true when we say "like father like son." There is no doubt that modelling is a powerful tool that parents and teachers can use to influence the development of positive behaviour in their children.

A child will model an adult's behaviour if the adult is someone the child respects. Parents and immediate family members are in this position exclusively in the early years of a child's development. It is very important before and during early school years that parents model the positive behaviours they want their children to adopt. The impact of the modelling may not be obvious immediately, although it should be evident in the future. The influence of parents is always strong although as the child grows, peers and the media tend to gain in influence. This illustrates how important it is for parents to be aware of the power of modelling early in the child's development. Remember *actions speak louder than words*. It is not enough to tell your child *"Do as I say"*. You must *practise what you preach* particularly early in development.

If a child is to experience success in school and develop a love of learning, parents must show, through their words and deeds, that they too, value these things. Show that you value school and learning by Involving yourself in your child's learning activities:

i.   Do some reading and writing together, on a regular basis, from infancy.

ii. Support your child's learning by being available whenever help is necessary.

iii. Work on assignments together, if this is appropriate- and act as a resource for your child.

iv. Consider continuing your education by enrolling in professional or general interest courses.

v. Talk positively about your school and the teachers who work there. Teacher and school bashing we read and hear about sends a very strong message to our children about how we view the school system. Even frequent references to school vacations or breaks, reinforce the feeling that school is something to be rid of. We rarely ask children if they are anxious to have their hockey season end or to stop going to their dance class, yet we reinforce the view that school is something kids should leave, wild with joy, at the end of June.

vi. Plan activities with your child that are fun and try to include some new learning experiences. Doing a wide variety of new activities provides learning opportunities simply because the activities might be first time experiences. Try some of these activities:

1. Attend children's theatre.
2. Visit the public library.
3. Visit the museum, a planetarium or an aquarium.
4. Take a trolley ride or a walking trip through the city.
5. Ride your bikes through a conservation area or park wilderness.
6. Together, design, create or build something.

Develop a family routine that has learning as the focus. Encourage and model pleasure reading at home, homework time, pursue hobbies or crafts, plan outings and watch programs of interest on educational television.

One critical element in successfully participating in any endeavour is understanding that success occurs when one puts forth the necessary effort. When children see their parents working hard each day, starting and sticking with a task until completed, they learn that hard work and effort have a direct bearing on success. As they mature the behaviours they have modelled will have an impact on how responsible they are for their own learning and their own success.

The Other Three Rs

Parenting is not an easy task. There are days when we feel we are making headway and other days when things seem to fall off the rails. To ensure these set backs are not permanent and long lasting, parents must create a certain relationship and a rapport that supports their children through difficult times.

It is important to create a home environment that is secure and provides the children with consistency. Children need to know they are loved unconditionally and supported through their rough times. Children need nurturing. Their talents need to be encouraged, their hurts, healed and their sadness, soothed. By providing these basic needs you are setting in place some of the ground work for successful personal interaction, a positive self-concept and future school success.

Behavioural expectations need to be set for all children. They need limits or guidelines about what is appropriate and acceptable to you. Setting limits tells them you care about them and how they behave. You will always have some rebellion against the rules and expectations you set. This is natural whether the child is a toddler *terrible twos or bossy threes* or a teenager. As your children grow peer influences become more important in their lives.

Children will test the limits you set to see how far they can go. They will push the limits of acceptable behaviour. Do not get discouraged. This is a normal part of growing up. Focus on why your guidelines are in the interest of the children and then persevere .

You might feel as if you and your rules are under siege or constantly being battered. Often, prohibiting your child from behaving in a certain way causes you some grief or guilt. There is a great deal of truth to the old adage that *This is going to hurt me more than it will hurt you.* It is important not to allow yourself to fall into this guilt trap. Externally, kids may want more freedom and fewer constraints on their behaviour. More importantly they need and want you to show you care about them by providing consistent expectations in a secure environment. As they grow, their sense of what constitutes appropriate behaviour will be affected by the rules you set for them as children.

In discussions with parents, teachers often comment on whether children are able to accept responsibilities for various tasks, such as completing assigned work, cleaning up after work or play, coming to class on time or being prepared with necessary materials. To a large degree, the responsibilities children are given at home affect the discipline and commitment necessary to accept responsibilities at school.

Starting Small: Thinking Big

Parents should assign an appropriate number of jobs, tasks or chores and then expect children to follow through on a regular basis for the benefit of the entire family. This helps develop a sense of self-discipline, commitment and contribution. The children will begin to see themselves as responsible and capable. This sense of self may then have a positive result when transferred to the school situation. The likelihood of taking responsibility for completing assignments, sharing clean-up tasks, bringing forms and letters home to parents, keeping the work area tidy and ultimately taking a responsible approach to learning is enhanced by being, from an early age, responsible at home. There are no perfect solutions when we discuss child- rearing and school success. The following guide-lines will give parents a starting point to develop The Other Three R's - Relationships, Rules and Responsibilities.

Tips to Enhance the Three Rs.

Building rapport and a positive relationship:
1. Read aloud to your children.
2. Play outdoor games like soccer, catch and hockey with your children.
3. Play quiet games like card games, Junior Monopoly or Scrabble.
4. Share secrets about positive things like birthday surprises for other family members.
5. Spend time talking about things that are important to you.

Five rules for setting guidelines:
1. Limit the amount and types of T.V. shows watched. Try "No T.V. Days".
2. Set limits on how far from your home your children can play.
3. Let them know the use of hurtful or negative words and behaviours are unacceptable in your family.
4. Set dinnertime rules such as "no one starts eating until all are ready to eat" or "no one leaves the table until parents say so".
5. A consistent bedtime is also very important.

Contributions to the family can be made through chores or tasks such as:
1. Setting the table and cleaning it off after meals.
2. Unloading the dishwasher or doing the dishes.
3. Making the bed every day and tidying the bedroom or playroom.
4. Putting out the trash.
5. Putting out and taking in the garbage can and recycling containers.

Know Where You Are Going

Most successful people set goals for themselves long before they achieve their success. Teachers often use goal setting to give children a focus in order to motivate them to higher academic achievement and improved social skills. Parents can also use this strategy to set personal, social and academic goals with their children. Certainly, the approach would vary with the age of the child involved. Setting a goal and then striving to reach it is a powerful motivator. This is an excellent way to give purpose or direction to a child, particularly if there is a reward involved.

It is important to decide specifically what you and your child want to achieve. What is the goal to be attained? Be realistic in your expectations. Setting too high a goal may result in frustration. Too low a goal can result in apathy. Regardless, both situations can cause the child to lose interest. Try to select a level that requires effort but one that the child sees as attainable.

Short term goals are best used with younger children and also for some older students who may need short term direction and focus. Some students can only deal with higher expectations for behaviour or achievement when those expectations are presented in small step approaches. Determine what is manageable for your child to handle and achieve successfully before you set the goal.

Involve your child in selecting the goal. If the child has some ownership in choosing the goal, then the chance of putting forth the necessary effort increases.

Once you decide on a goal you must determine what you need to do to get there. Write down some specific strategies, or things to do, in order to be successful. Be specific about what will be done, when, how and by whom. What part will your child play and what will you do to support? This can be as complex or as simple as you would like. Simple is more manageable and meaningful for children. Depending on the child's age, you may want to post the goal and the strategies so that they are always visible and easily remembered. Writing the goal and the strategies as a contract to be signed and copied for all concerned is another very powerful option. The support role a parent provides is crucial. The parent needs to determine how much support in the form of verbal encouragement, discussion, problem solving or material, is necessary.

Periodically, evaluate the success of the strategies you have chosen. If you find things are not progressing as planned you may have to change the activities or the time needed to be successful. Be flexible, but always keep your goal in mind.

Reinforcement is something that all children need. Remember to encourage your child and maintain high expectations. Achievement of goals is never a perfect or precise process, therefore, be realistic about successes and setbacks. As long as the child is moving forward, be happy.

Five Common School Goals:
1. Arrive on time prepared for class.
2. Complete a specific assignment on time
3. Achieve a high mark in a certain subject.
4. Learn a new social skill such as taking turns, encouraging others or listening carefully.
5. Listen carefully when the teacher is giving instructions or presenting a lesson.

Five Goals For The Home:
1. Read everyday.
2. Make your bed and tidy your room everyday.
3. Brush your teeth, comb your hair and wash your face everyday.
4. Put all your toys away at the end of the day.
5. Co-operate with the babysitter.

Communication: The Basis For Learning

A school is a social environment and success in this environment is measured in different areas. Certainly academic success, or learning, is of paramount importance. One of the reasons our schools exist is to provide children with a high level of knowledge and skills. The development of positive social skills is also a very important goal.

Success in school is affected by the child's ability to communicate, in other words, to read, write, speak and listen. Early involvement by parents to develop communication skills should enhance academic and social success.

The child's ability to communicate effectively is evident to teachers and students very early in the formal school years. How children see themselves and how other students and teachers see them, affects their achievement. Children need to see themselves as capable. In grade one this might mean being able to identify all the letters of the alphabet, spell many words properly or be able to answer correctly addition and subtraction questions. In grade four, it might mean being able to answer questions about animals, plants or geography and do so in group discussions. Those children who believe they can answer correctly, will do so most of the time. Their peers will see them giving correct answers or having a rich background knowledge and therefore will come to expect this from them.

Parents and teachers are aware of the impact of the self-fulfilling prophesy. It is important that the self-fulfilling prophecy be positive for every child. This is made possible if adults view every child in a positive light and if all children see themselves as capable. By following some of the strategies listed in the following pages, parents should help their child's early school experiences be positive.

The individuality of each child is recognized and promoted by teachers and schools. To some degree socialization in school means losing some of this individuality and fitting in, or conforming. Fitting in and the acceptance this offers is important to children not only when playing outside at recess but also in class. Everyone wants to be asked to play and not to be picked last when choosing teams. As well, children want to answer questions and take part in class discussions with the knowledge that teachers and peers accept and value their contributions. With a head start, or enhanced communication skills, at an early age, children should have an easier time fitting in and gaining peer acceptance. As well, with effective communication skills, children may find their individual choices increased. Their capabilities in language, social studies, mathematics and other subject areas will be recognized by classmates.

Entering school with a good basis for further developing reading, writing, speaking and listening, results in positive peer and teacher interaction. This can be very helpful in maintaining a happy, productive child and a successful school experience.

Discipline Begins at Home

Parents and community groups are very concerned about the increasing incidence of school yard violence. School Boards are now producing policies and procedures to deal with these situations. The most significant impact on improving discipline at school can be made by teaching discipline, at an early age, at home.

The goal of any discipline program should be to teach children to become responsible and self-disciplined. Discipline and punishment are not synonymous. To simply punish children for bad choices in behaviour is not productive. It is important that children understand that certain consequences result from certain actions, and as responsible individuals they need to accept the consequences of their actions. For example if a child:

1. Does not complete homework, an appropriate consequence would be to stay at school after dismissal to complete the work and possibly miss another activity.

2. Breaks another child's toy or other possession an appropriate consequence would be to replace or repair the damaged item and apologize.

Although the consequences listed above are reactions to negative behaviours parents can take the positive, or pro-active, approach. Presenting children with desirable consequences for positive behaviour strengthens the likelihood this good behaviour will reoccur.

The consequence that results from inappropriate behaviour should be seen as fair, in other words neither too extreme nor lenient. The consequence should be consistent, or applied the same way for each person in each instance. Children have a very strong sense of fairness and if they do not think they are being dealt with fairly they will speak up increasingly as they grow. It is important to apply the consequence immediately after the misbehaviour and if possible, it should relate to the misbehaviour. Finally, the consequence should be applied calmly to show that you are in control of the situation. You must respond in a firm manner to show that you disapprove. Children may try to explain why they should not be subjected to any consequence at all. Often parents must walk a tight rope when determining how much support to give their child when misbehaviour has occured at school. If the school determines a consequence, parents must take care not to bail out the child and communicate the message that one does not have to accept the consequences of inappropriate behaviour.

To reduce misbehaviour, parents should to talk with their children about empathy, understanding how others feel. Exploring specific strategies for controlling anger and for solving problems is also very important. Schools try to do this by using anti-violence curriculum such as the *Second*

Step program. This program was developed by the Committee for Children in Seattle, Washington. Other materials, often produced locally for specific needs, are also used. When a discipline situation occurs the following consequences may be useful, with some variation, for the specific problem:

1. An apology.
2. Removal of privileges such as lose television time, or snacks before or after dinner.
3. Isolation, commonly called grounding.
4. Restitution - replacement or repair.
5. Community service - a clean-up or work time to rectify the situation.
6. Loss of toys or other items.
7. Use of a combination of the above. All these consequences are reactions to unacceptable behaviour.

Parents should also consider the pro-active approach, in other words, do specific things that will prevent problem behaviours in children. The following ideas are some important suggestions to encourage good behaviour:

1. Talk with your children and listen carefully to what they are saying.
2. Spend time with your children engaged in positive activities such as games, sports or school work. If possible, this is even more powerful if it is one-to-one time without interruptions by other siblings.
3. Give your children rewards, whether material or verbal, for consistently positive behaviour, for appropriate periods of time. One of the greatest rewards is one-on-one time with you.

4. In your discussions with your children, make sure you discuss not only individual rights but responsibilities, including respect for other people's rights. Too often in our schools we have students who are well aware of their rights but give little thought to the rights of others.

There is no single way to reduce negative behaviour and increase positive behaviour in children. This is a long term process, involving the use of different strategies to encourage good behaviour while building a relationship of mutual love and respect. It is important to remember to support your child with rewards or consequences that will achieve the desired result.

The More You Do...The More You Can Do

Success in an activity is related to the commitment a person has when performing that activity. If success in school is the goal then involvement by the student and parent will enhance this success. This involvement should create in children and parents a sense of ownership or responsibility for learning.

Once your children begin formal schooling encourage them to become involved in school clubs, groups or teams. Generally, there may be few school teams or clubs for students in the primary grades (K-gr.2) therefore, parents may want to look at involving their children in activities such as soccer, t-ball, cubs, brownies, swimming, dancing or musical lessons, run by organizations in the community. Once children reach grade 3 the number of sports and clubs available at school tends to increase. Whether the activity is short term or year round, a school team or intramural, the important thing is that the children are involved, follow through on a commitment and make a positive contribution.

Involvement builds character. Being a part of a group gives children a sense of belonging and enhances the positive light in which they view themselves. Involvement also enhances the way children are viewed by peers. This alone has an increasing importance for their social and emotional well being, particularly as puberty approaches.

Involvement in clubs or groups may also enhance physical qualities. Sports enhance the fitness and athletic skills (throwing, catching, running, jumping) of children and allow them to perform at a higher level. Musical, dancing or dramatic activities also allow children to learn new skills and develop the artistic qualities that all children possess.

The physical, artistic and emotional benefits children obtain from involvement can influence their interaction with others. Working and getting along with other people becomes exceedingly important as children go on in school. Being part of one or more groups at school allows the student to become familiar with other students and teachers. Friends are made and the comfort level in group situations increases. Children also learn to model some of the positive behaviours involved in team work. The social skills necessary to get along with others may also be improved.

The extent to which children are involved in school clubs, groups or teams may increase confidence, self-esteem, acceptance and success in social situations. The result should be happier students who see themselves as capable and, therefore, rise to a level of school success that reflects their abilities.

Children Solving Conflicts

We all have occasions when we are in conflict with someone else, either a family member, a friend or a collegue. Solving these conflicts or disagreements is difficult for adults. Imagine the difficulty children face! They have not had the experience nor developed the skills needed to work through a conflict situation. As a result children often experience unnecessary stress and anxiety over a specific situation or one they think may occur.

The stress children feel from conflict situations will always have some impact on other areas of their lives. Children need reassurance that they can deal with any situation that arises. They need to be encouraged to see themselves as capable problem solvers. Parents and other significant adults must teach children the skills necessary to solve conflicts.

As your children grow the foundation for successful conflict resolution will develop. Here are eight strategies to help your children solve conflicts:
1. Teach your children to share. Many cultures stress this concept and the benefits it brings for individuals and society. Sharing possessions and experiences helps to reduce conflicts.

2. Learning to take turns is important. This affects children during work and play situations. To a child, taking turns means *your way this time, my way next time.*

3. Sometimes a child must give something in order to get something back. The idea of **compromise** will help the child learn to negotiate in order to solve, or diffuse, a conflict.

4. Occasionally when children have a disagreement the solution may be as simple as a **flip of a coin.** *Heads I win, tails you win.* Each child has an equal chance of winning though there is clearly a winner and a loser.

5. If the problems are involved and difficult to solve, children should be aware that seeking some **outside help** is appropriate. A parent , teacher, coach or friend might be helpful in mediating, diffusing or solving a conflict.

6. Problems do not always require an immediate solution. If the child is not sure what to do it might be appropriate to take some time to think about the situation and make a **decision** at another time.

7. **Avoiding** the problem will not solve it but it will reduce conflict situations. It is not unusual for parents and teachers to advise children who can not resolve their problems to stay away from each other. With respect as a cornerstone, children should realize that simply agreeing to disagree could be the solution.

8. Humour can prevent and diffuse conflict situations. The humour must not be at the other person's expense but rather provide something that all those involved can laugh about.

Whether children or adults are involved, a solution is always possible if we keep an open mind. Listening carefully to what the other person is saying can help us understand how they are feeling.

Starting Small: Thinking Big

For some students success in school happens with relative ease. For others, it is more a product of effort and hard work. Success always depends on a number of different factors or influences coming together at the right time. By laying the necessary foundation and reinforcing certain behaviours, parents can play a very important role in preparing their child for school success.

Here are some suggestions that should help your children have a successful school experience:

1. **Start early.** Read to your children on a regular basis from infancy. As they get older have them read to you. Eventually include writing as part of your time together. Children's readiness for reading and writing will increase and the affection, security and warmth experienced during your story-times will further your own relationship.

2. **Develop routines** for your entire family that encourage learning activities. As much as possible set aside the same time every day when all family members read, write or do some activity related to learning.

3. Give your children responsibilities that are suitable and expect them to follow through. Making their beds, tidying their rooms, vacuuming or taking out the trash are all appropriate. This should build a responsible approach to work and enhance their self-concept as they see themselves as capable, trustworthy individuals.

4. Spend time regularly involved in varied activities with your children. Whether going to little league, the zoo or the theatre, all these activities help develop vocabulary and increase children's background knowledge. These experiences will be very helpful when developing reading and writing skills. The fact that you have shared these experiences should also help to strengthen the bond between you.

5. Appropriate discipline has always been a topic that generates a lot of discussion. Different people approach it in different ways. Very early on children will learn what type of behaviour you expect, what you will put-up with and what they can get away with. It is important to show your children in a firm, consistent and loving way that you mean what you say. Children, whether toddlers or teens, will try to wear down their parents. If you make a reasoned decision,be firm and approach discipline with a consist-ent, caring nature. If you can do this, the message you give will be one that promotes responsible behaviour, high expectations and self-esteem.

6. Setting reasonable expectations is important. Your children will, in most cases, rise to meet the expectations you set, although they will tend to give you what they have learned you will accept. Once you set a high expectation it is important to support your children so they can attain the desired level. Remember that the self-fullfilling prophecy is real, so set your expectations wisely. Be careful not to set an expectation that is unreachable, but one that is attainable with perseverance and hard work.

7. Communication is of prime importance to your child's success. It's always best to go to the source to confirm your information. Information passed from teacher to child to parent and visa versa is, at best, not complete and frequently inaccurate, with the intent and context completely missing. Speak directly to your child's teacher - and not only at interview time - for information about program needs, social skills and what you can do to help. Do your part to prevent misinformation.

8. Be positive about school, learning and the concept of education for life. Talk about the necessity and merits of school. Give your children a positive impression of schooling. Do not denigrate schools, the school system or individuals. Your child will quickly learn how you feel about school and education. If you want your children to develop a positive attitude toward school and learning then talk positively with them about school.

9. **Encourage** your children's educational endeavours and allow them to learn from mistakes they might make at school. Let them know that is part of the experience of life and what is really important is what they do with the knowledge they gain from these experiences. Allow them, within reason, to suffer or accept the consequences of their actions. Do not bail them out. Ultimately they will see themselves as more responsible and capable learners.

10. T.V. is one of the best sedatives ever discovered. Monitor and limit your children's television viewing. They will put up a fuss but it is in their best interest to be involved in other activities that stimulate creativity, imagination and social and intellectual skills. Violence on television is often quickly modelled by children and can impact on social interaction at school. If you find this becoming an issue take a closer look at the television shows your children watch.

11. Remember that **actions speak louder than words**. Model the behaviours you want from your children. *Do as I say, not as I do* is no longer effective in the ever changing world of infinite choices, influences and distractions.

Learning
With Style

By knowing your child's primary method of obtaining information from the environment, or learning style, you can influence future school success. Teachers use information about learning styles to plan student programs and create a positive learning environment for each child. Knowledge of individual learning styles helps teachers understand student behaviours and modify programs to meet individual learning needs. Parents can also use this knowledge to understand their children and deal with them in ways that enhance their learning.

Researchers have identified four learning styles: *kinesthetic, tactile, auditory and visual*. Students receive information about their environment through all these channels although one style is usually more dominant than the others. Knowing which style is dominant for a student can give a parent and teacher information about how the student learns best.

If you have found your child to be active, impulsive, someone who loves hands-on projects, you may have a *kinesthetic learner* in your home. The term kinesthetic refers to the fact that the child learns by doing. Knowledge or skill is understood after an activity has been completed.

These children often excel in sports and physical activities. They rarely read for pleasure though they will read for meaning and information. Teachers often recognize them by their illegible handwriting. These children tend to be poor test-takers.

Parents and teachers can help these children by encouraging them and finding ways for them to apply what they have learned. It is important for them to work in small groups in order to get the attention they need. For this group of learners their actions definitely speak louder than their words.

Children who focus on non-verbal communication and its meaning are called *tactile learners*. They have a clear understanding of people's moods and feelings. These children are very aware of their environment. In class they are often very neat writers. They have special sensitivity to the classroom environment, where they sit, and even the amount of light and noise level are all important factors for them.

These students can be helped in their learning by parents and teachers who are caring, nurturing and whose actions extend invitations to learn. It is important to build rapport in order to help these children. Once this occurs, the respect the child has for the adult will enhance his or her openness to learning. These students do not care what you know until they know that you care.

You will recognize the *auditory learner* because this is the student who is always talking. This person talks and talks and does not care about the rules. In order for these children to understand information they must read it, talk about it and hear it. In school we often see these children with their hands up all the time, straining to be called upon when the teacher asks questions. During testing situations these students may have difficulty if there is a set time limit.

Parents and teachers can help these students learn by understanding their need to speak and therefore not forcing them to be quiet when learning. It is important to provide ample opportunities for discussion so they can hear themselves thinking. The information these students learn needs to be heard not seen.

Visual learners are the students most suited to the traditional classroom. These students need a quiet environment in which to work. They want their information written down. When they study for tests they review the notes they have made. These children learn best by seeing the information. For them the picture is truly worth 1000 words.

When dealing with issues in education rarely is a topic black or white. We learn best in one particular style though there will be situations when we will be expected to work under conditions that stress another, less preferred, approach. Regardless, we are also able to learn using other styles of learning.

With some awareness of your child's preferred learning style you should be able to help your child with school work and arrange appropriate experiences that enhance learning outside the classroom.

Flaherty, Geraldine, *The Learning Curve: Why Textbook Teaching Doesn't Work For All Kids*. Vocational Education Journal, Alexandria, Va. USA. 1992.

Concrete Steps To Learning

Learning is a complex process. Children acquire knowledge through their own experiences and through structured lessons presented by a teacher or parent. Often, when a child is first exposed to a skill or concept, the learning occurs quickly. Some children may need further reinforcement and exposure in order to fully understand the material. Since children learn at different rates and in their own way, they may require information to be presented in different ways. Good teachers know that presenting information to children (a) in a concrete, (b) a pictorial or (c) an abstract sequence can help enhance their learning.

The use of the concrete, pictorial and abstract approach to teach children is an effective way to help them understand. Many students need to hold, manipulate, move and organize solid, or concrete, objects before they can understand a concept or learn a new skill.

This sequence of presenting information is appropriate although depending on the child's level of development and understanding, a teacher will have to determine what needs reteaching and which type of presentation is most effective.

Having material presented in a pictorial fashion, using diagrams, that relate to the material being learned helps make the information more clear and meaningful for many children.

Presenting information in an abstract fashion, through discussion, writing or numbers is fine for many children but most will need the concrete and/or pictorial approach first inorder to learn new skills or ideas.

For a number of reasons teachers and parents may want to be aware of these three approaches to teaching. The use of all or part of this sequence for learning helps ensure that all learners are able to understand, regardless of their level of development. Teachers have found that getting children actively involved in an activity through use of concrete materials and pictures helps to motivate students by removing some of the drudgery from strictly pencil and paper tasks. These tasks have their place when used in conjunction with other strategies.

Mathematics is one subject where good teachers rely heavily on concrete materials. The use of little wooden cubes, beans or marbles helps children understand the concept of numbers. Teachers also use these objects to help their students understand the concept and skill of regrouping, borrowing and carrying, in addition and subtraction.

Telling time is often something children begin learning at home. Teachers reinforce this skill at school through the use of cardboard or wooden clock faces which children can manipulate. The wall clock at home is also a concrete object that parents can use. The next step at school is generally to have the students draw the hands of the clock onto pictures of clock faces. There are many commercial products available that parents can purchase for home use. Sometimes it is more fun and practical to use things found at home or make your own. The use of concrete or manipulative materials helps children understand initial mathematics concepts so they can apply them more effectively in the future.

Science and environmental studies teachers know the value of using concrete materials. Children love to explore the natural environment, to collect stones, leaves, plants and observe insects and larger animals. Children need personal experience with their environment through objects they can manipulate, pictorial images and carefully selected and planned field trips.

To stimulate or encourage writing, language teachers often use objects and large pictures that relate to the topic or theme being studied. This helps make the real- world connection for the children and gives them more experience that they can draw on for their writing.

If your child is having difficulty with a concept or a skill, you may want to think about how the use of concrete objects and pictorial representations can help. Try explaining the material using something concrete. Have the child touch, move,sort, describe or manipulate the objects then go back to discuss the information once more. You may have to use a number of examples or situations to reinforce. The use of concrete or pictorial materials is not a panacea but it should help to enhance your child's understanding and skills.

Asking Questions

Questions stimulate learning. We learn by answering questions and from the thinking involved in arriving at the answer. The types of questions we ask children require them to think in different ways.

Questions vary in complexity and therefore the complexity of the thinking required for the answer also varies. Lower level or less complex types of questions include the typical *Who? What? When? Where?* questions. On the other hand higher level, or more complex, questions go beyond simply recalling or identifying facts, to using information, evaluating it and creating a new use or purpose for the information.

Researchers have found that the type of question asked is related to the type of thinking required to answer. Parents and teachers can enhance children's learning by becoming more familiar with the various levels and types of questions and by asking a wide variety of questions when working with children.

The most basic level of questioning require the student to simply recall or recognize facts. These questions typically begin with *Who? What? When? Where?* Questions that require a student to *Tell, State, Define or Name* are also examples of basic knowledge questions. In many cases traditional testing methods have focussed primarily at this level. There is a place for these types of questions although parents need to be aware of their use and use them as part of a larger variety of questions on which they draw.

The next group of questions raises the level of thinking by requiring the student to show an understanding of what has been taught and an ability to use the information. Questions in this category require students to interpret, analyse and apply information they have learned. Typically some questions that require this type of thinking may begin with *Why? Explain, Compare, and Discuss.* Parents can use these types of questions to help their children with homework or on any occasion when the goal is to understand certain information.

The highest level of questioning requires the student to give opinions, make judgments and use information in creative ways. These types of questions are referred to as open-ended because they have no right or wrong answer. The student may be required to support an opinion or decision . Some questions at this level begin with *What if...? How would...? Design, Create or Which do you prefer?*

Questions direct and enhance thinking. Using a variety of questions at different levels will require children to think in different ways in order to answer successfully. If parents and teachers want to raise the level of children's thinking, knowledge of questioning will help them phrase questions appropriately.

Performance Learning Systems Inc., *Professional Refinements in Developing Effectiveness*. Emerson N.J. USA. 1980.

Sanders, Norris M., *Classroom Questions: What Kinds?* New York, N.Y. Harper Collins College. 1978

Reading Brings Lifelong Payoffs

It is very important that parents spend time engaged in nurturing experiences with their children. One of the most important skills you can teach is how to communicate effectively. Children's ability to communicate will influence their relationships, school success and career opportunities. Regular reading will enhance your children's communication skills.

The interest you show in reading and the importance you place upon it will be evident to your children. Reading aloud will help them learn new vocabulary and experience new situations. Reading together also provides opportunities to experience love, warmth and security when a child snuggles up to read a new book with Mom or Dad.

Reading aloud also acts as a motivator. It allows children to recognize new words and hear them being used properly. This experience will help when they begin to read alone.

Listening is an important part of communicating. As you describe the characters and the events, they will be tuning into your voice inflections, intonation, pauses and stresses.

When you are reading your children will be learning the importance of listening.

Reading aloud enhances linguistic level, or the ability to speak properly. As children hear more and more words used appropriately their own vocabulary and knowledge of word use will increase. They will begin using words they have learned through your oral reading. This method of vocabulary development is far better than flash cards or drills. Reading to your children ultimately helps them to become better speakers.

Reading helps to increase comprehension or under-standing of information. Books provide opportunities for children to experience different situations, locations, characters and problems. With more experiences, either real or read, they should find it easier to understand new words and reading material.

Stratagies For Reading Aloud

When a parent or other significant adult reads aloud to a child the benefits are many and can be far reaching. The emotional relationship between the parent and child is enhanced by the time spent reading and talking about a story. The child learns by example, to value reading and the learning associated with it. Reading aloud also enhances the child's ability to read and can have a positive effect on emotional, and future academic, well-being.

Reading to children is a regular routine for many parents. Parents of toddlers should also consider reading aloud to their little ones. This is certainly not a difficult or complicated task although focussing a child's attention and directing the thinking makes the reading more meaningful and enjoyable. Following is a list of ideas and reading strategies for parents or other adult readers to consider when reading to children:

1.   Involve the child when reading material is chosen. Children love to choose new books and books they have heard and read many times before. They may choose a favourite story classic or something more current about a familiar television, movie or cartoon character. If a child

shows an interest in a certain theme or series of books capitalize on this while including some of your own selections to provide a wide variety.

2. Preview the book that you are going to read. Look over the cover design and the pictures or diagrams inside. Ask the child some questions and answer others that may arise. This will give the child some initial familiarity with the story.

3. Read with feeling and enthusiasm. Read the lines the way the characters would speak them. There is no need to exaggerate although reading expressively makes the story more enjoyable and teaches the child the importance of expression, voice inflection, intonation and their importance in conveying a message.

4. Take turns reading. With beginning readers this is an excellent way to reinforce their skills. Read a short passage, from one sentence to one paragraph, and then have the child read it back to you. The child will model your reading and new or difficult words will be easier to read after they have been heard.

A variation of this strategy involves reading a brief passage and then having the child read the next few sentences. This pattern simply repeats itself. Of course this would be more appropriate for children who are further along in their reading development.

5. Children love to hear their favourite stories over and over again. Although the parent may wish to read something else the child eagerly awaits that tattered old book that has been read one hundred times. This may explain children's enthusiasm for stories with repetitive text or a pattern to the writing. Poetry books such as *Where The Sidewalk Ends* by Shel Silverstein and other books with reoccurring words or phrases such as the Dr. Suess books offer the repetition helpful to beginning readers.

6. Use context clues to help with difficult words.
i.   If the child is reading and comes to a difficult or new word ask a question like, "What do you think would fit there?" Give a clue and then ask the child to respond, for example, "Since this happened earlier in the story what do you think the little girl would do now?"
ii.   Briefly give some information from the sections read previously to give the child more perspective and then ask the child to select a word that would fit.
iii.   Most books for beginning readers and older children include many pictures or drawings that depict scenes from the story. If a child comes to a difficult word or section focus their attention on the artwork and ask them to make decision about what would fit best in the specific case.
iv.   If a difficult word appears and it has been read before have the child try to recall a word read before, with the same beginning letter in a similar context.
v.   Another method used by teachers to determine a child's understanding of a story is called *Cloze*. This strategy involves taking a passage and removing every

tenth word. The child would then read the passage and substitute, in each blank, a word that makes sense and shows the child understands what is being read. This technique can be used to help children focus, and improve, their understanding. There is some work involved in preparing a passage for use in this fashion.

7. Use phonetic, or letter sound, clues to decode words.
i. Most of us remember how we were taught to sound out the word. Ask the child who has difficulty "What is the first letter?" "What sound does it make?" "What is the last letter?" "What sound does the ending make?" Have the child try putting all the sounds together to form the word.
ii. Give the child a difficult word such as "rhymes with..." or "sounds like..." and give some clues without giving the actual word.
iii. Give the child a clue about the meaning of the word. You could say, "It means the same as...," or "It is the opposite of ..."
iv. Break the word into syllables or find small more familiar words within the larger compound words. Highlight these smaller words, individual sounds and endings to pronounce the difficult word.

8. Another strategy to determine a child's understanding of the reading involves asking the child to **predict** what will happen next. This will bring another element of fun and discussion into the reading.

All individuals need encouragement in order to continue an activity and improve their performance. Children are especially influenced by positive comments and suggestions made by a nurturing, caring adult. When you read with your child remember to maintain the positive nature of the reading. Do not get bogged down or belabour the pronunciation of individual words. By correcting every single word or mistake the child makes, you will make the reading disjointed and a negative and frustrating experience. Children who experience regular frustration will not be inclined to continue reading for pleasure. They begin to see themselves as incapable of becoming good readers.

Maintaining a positive, fun approach to reading aloud will pay personal and academic dividends for the child. By using a variety of strategies and focussing the child's attention the results should be even greater.

Taking The "Numb" Out Of Numbers

Taking the "numb" out of numbers is something parents can help ensure by encouraging their children's interest in mathematics at an early age. Creative and inspiring teachers do this although parent influence can be more long lasting and consistent. Girls have tended not to go on in mathematics or science beyond high school. In many cases their achievement in these areas has tended to lag behind boys. As a result, it is very important to encourage boys and girls equally when discussing or doing activities related to mathematics or science. Science activities are included because they are closely related to mathematics. As always, it is important for children to see and hear their parents talking in a positive way about mathematics and science. Children will pick-up very quickly whether these subjects are thought of as onerous, difficult and unimportant. They are exactly the opposite, and this perception is an important determinant of how children achieve.

The mathematics programs in elementary school are usually comprised of the following areas:

1. Numbers (counting, computation).

2. Measurement (estimate and measure time, distance, mass, volume, area).

3. Geometry (two and three dimensional shapes).

4. Problem solving (using all other mathematics skills to answer questions and solve problems).

Parents often have opportunities to work with their children on homework assignments that relate to the different topics. Parents can use the following strategies to help their children feel comfortable with mathematics and see the connection between what goes on in the elementary classroom and the real world. Try the following suggestions to help take the "numb" out of numbers:

1. Play games that provide counting practise or use dice. Games like *Snakes and Ladders* or *Junior Monopoly*" are useful. Count everything. Count by ones, twos, fives, tens and hundreds. Look for patterns in counting, adding and subtracting numbers.

2. Buy your children their own calculator or electronic mathematics games like those produced by *Texas Instruments*.

3. Give your children rulers. Measure and have them keep track of their growth. Have them measure, for fun, other objects around your home. Use a bathroom scale to measure their mass. Remember to review the units of

measurement and have the children estimate before actually measuring. This will allow them to practice this skill and help them to check the accuracy of the measurement.

4. Teach your children common two and three dimensional shapes. When you are travelling or when the opportunity arises have them identify the shapes of buildings, other structures and in objects occurring naturally.

5. Involve children in solving simple problems that require some mathematics skills. The following examples are some possible mathematics problems:
a. How much a child has grown?
b. How much change you will get when something is purchased?
c. Using appropriate quantities of ingredients for baking.
d. Which shapes are commonly found around your house?

Making mathematics relevant and fun for young children and ensuring there is support when difficulties arise should help to strengthen enjoyment and future achievement in mathematics.

Regular Homework: A Key To School Success

Homework is one of the topics parents most often ask teachers about. Questions such as "Should my child be doing homework?" "How much homework is apporoprate?" "How can I help?" are asked regularly at parent-teacher conferences. Research in this area clearly indicates that students who do regular homework perform on a higher level in school than students who do little or no regular homework. Learning can no longer be limited to work done at school. It is important for children to maintain their learning in all facets of their lives, school, play and home.

Homework for the school aged child can begin immediately after entering school. For kindergarten and first grade students homework may involve a parent reading and discussing a story with the child, counting, playing a number or word game or drawing. As the child progresses through school the complexity of the homework increases.

As a rule, about five minutes of homework is recomended for each grade the child has been in.(eg. grade two, ten minutes, grade eight, 40 minutes).

Students may wish to spend more time depending on their interest and the complexity of the homework.

It is important, particularly for younger children, to recognnize that play provides many opportunites for learning and socialization. Appropriate time should be provided for both play and homework.

Parents have an important role to play in helping their children do homework. The following are ten important things that parents can do to help their children: 1/Do the homework; 2/ Improve the quality fo the final product; 3/ Develop a routine for self-directed homework and study.

1. The first question a parent should ask is "Where will my child do the homework?" The work area must be appropriate for learning. The student should have a desk and a comfortable chair, proper lighting, pens, paper, markers, and other materials. A work area should be set-up so the student can go to the same location every day. Many of us may remember doing our homework at the kitchen table. This too may be appropriate depending on the child's learning style.

2. Once the work area has been set-up, for many children, it is important to remove distractions such as noise, television, telephone interruptions or too may activities in the immediate area. Distractions may cause the student to shift the focus of attention resulting in less concentration and less learning. On the other hand

because of the variety of learning styles some children find that they need a homework environment that is more flexible, more relaxed with routine distractions such as music, background noise, food and interruptions for breaks or discussion. The child's favoured learning style should certainly be considered.

3. Develop a household routine that focusses on a homework schedule for everyone in the family. You should set aside some time each day possibly right after school or just after dinner.

4. In order to be sucessful at any task it is important to clearly understand what is expected. Have your children tell you in their own works what the assignment is. Make sure they know what to do and how to get started. If you maintain regular contact with your children's teacher you will have a good idea of what is required and where the homework is leading.

5. As always *actions speak louder than words*. Sit with your children during the homework, particularly at the start. It is not always possible or necessary to stay for the entire time but let them know that your are available for questions and guidance. Remember to be patient. It is often more difficult to be patient with one's own children than with someone else's.

6. When your children come to you with questions it is important to respond so as to direct their investigation

without simply giving the answer. You must judge whether to answer specifically or how much of the answer to give. Try answering the question with another question to focus the thinking. Questions asking what the child thinks or probing questions encourage the student to answer without being told explicitly. There may also be more than one correct answer so leave the door open to more than one interpretation.

7. Good teachers use a variety of skills and strategies to raise the level of their students' thinking. You can also elevate your child's thought processes. The types of questions you ask should require different levels of response or thinking. Look for situations to ask a variety of questions that touch on different levels of thinking. Questions beginning with *Who, What, When, and Where*, generally involve a lower level of thinking in the area of basic knowledge and recall. Questions which stimulate higher levels of thinking require students to apply, evaluate and sythesize information. These questions might be phrased as follows: *What is..How would you...Evaluate the success of...* One of the easiest and most effective ways to get your child thinking on a higher level is to ask a variety of questions requiring some application, evaluation and creative use of information.

8. Research has shown that a great deal of learning takes place when a student is required to teach someone else what has been learned. Have your child teach you the homework.

9. All homework has a deadline. Teach your children that they are responsible for completing the work on time and that the due date must be met. Over time this approach will teach them to be disciplined and reponsible learners.

10. Set high expectations for your children. Expect success and with your support they will rise to meet your expectations.

There is no single or simple way of achieving success with homework. Using some of the strategies suggested in your particular situation should help to create a learning environment that will promote success and a positive attitude toward learning.

Successful Test Preparation

At some point every student will take part in tests which evaluate their progress or success in achieving certain skills or knowledge.

Evaluation of student progress takes many forms in today's classroom. The use of ongoing evaluation of classroom work, group work, problem-solving assignments, research projects and teacher observation are some of the more common strategies used today. Teacher designed tests are also used, to varying degrees, when determining term or final marks for older students. Generally, for younger students, the emphasis is placed on shorter, more frequent, quizzes that deal with specific skills or concepts, ongoing observations and regular evaluation of daily work.

The best way to ensure a high degree of understanding and skill development is to maintain ongoing review of the material covered in class. Children should stay on task when in class, avoid distractions and be actively involved in their learning. Being focussed in class should help them attain good results during the ongoing evaluation and at test time.

Starting Small: Thinking Big

If you need to help your children review for a test you can do a number of things to help them increase their chance of success. Try some of the following strategies:

1. Find out what information you will need to know. What topics will be covered? What format will the test take? This information will help your child focus the preparation and allow for the best use of time.

2. Have your child **read** over all their notes and other material given to them by the teacher. If you know what the test will cover focus the reading and review the appropriate material. Highlight important information in the notes by use of a highlight marker or pen.

3. Write out some important questions and then write out the answers. This will provide an opportunity to reflect on what is important for this test.

4. Write out the notes. Some students improve their recall by writing out important information. Prepare a summary of information or ideas that are important.

5. If your child is writing a mathematics test have them do a number of questions that show they understand how to apply a certain skill or solution.

6. Have your child work with a family member or friend. Solve some problems and answer some questions together. Quiz each other.

7. Have your child **teach** you what they have learned. This is an excellent way to strengthen their knowledge.

8. **Practise. Practise. Practise.**

9. Make sure your child **rests** and eats properly. Drowsiness and hunger during a test can create significant problems.

Everyone has their own learning style and their own particular way of preparing for testing. Over time you will find what works best for your child. Regular ongoing review will help reduce anxiety and the need for intensive study at test taking time.

Your child's frame of mind is also very important. Children must believe in their ability to succeed. Some stress may even enhance their performance. Too much worry can result in poor test results. With good test preparation and regular review your child should be able to handle effectively any testing situation.

The Key to Successful Parent Teacher Conferences

Every year parents receive report cards which outline the progress their children have made during each term.

Although there may be differences in the types of report cards used, the purpose is the same. The report card is intended to give parents information about their child's academic progress.

Teachers will usually include information about children's academic strengths and areas where improvement is necessary.

Although schools attempt to make report cards easy to understand, the parent-teacher interview can help to explain, in more detail, the child's academic and social development. By spending a few minutes preparing for the parent-teacher interview you will learn more specific information about your child. Here are a few ideas to consider before your meeting:

1. **Read the report card** carefully and write down any questions you have about specific remarks or comments. Comments and marks on report cards generally reflect the achievement of knowledge and skills learning outcomes, work habits and behaviour.

You may want to ask questions about these areas. Social interaction is very important to a child's success at school. Children often behave differently at school than they do at home. Get the teacher's perspective on your child's ability to make and keep friends and how he/she relates in group situations. An unhappy child will not be a productive child.

2. During the interview, ask questions about how your child was evaluated. Teachers use various methods. Seeing samples of work can help give you a good picture of progress. If you are familiar with these techniques you may be better able to help your child with school work next term.

3. If necessary, determine a plan of action with the teacher. What will be done during the next term to help your child with those areas in language and mathematics, where further development is needed? Set a check back time when you and the teacher can evaluate what has been done and determine what else needs doing.

4. If there is something you need clarified, just ask the teacher. If educational jargon creeps into the discussion, point it out. Communication is very important to a child's success in school.

5. Remember that both you and the teacher have your child's well-being in mind. It is important that you work together.

You may not agree with each other on every point but if you keep an open mind, solutions are possible. Remember to listen, for both of you have an important perspective to share. Focus on the academic and social issues surrounding your child's progress at school and what you can do together to keep it going.

Building For
The Future

During May or June, most schools begin the process of forming classes for the next school year. Although classes are often not finalized until late August, the process and discussion begins much earlier. Although some might think otherwise, a great deal of thought goes into class building. Teachers know the student's academic and social needs. They base their decisions about class placement on their perception of what would create the best learning environment for each child. This is the basic objective of the class building process.

In order to create good class groupings, the teachers and the school, must look at the big picture. In other words, when looking at specific criteria for placement teachers also consider how the child would respond in the larger group situation.

Class forming is a co-operative effort involving the teachers of the present grade with the teachers assigned to the next grade in September. This group considers very basic criteria such as boy/girl ratio and more complex details, such as specific program issues. The following information is also considered: the student's learning style, the teacher's style of teaching, class size, previous information is also considered: the student's learning style, the teacher's style of teaching, class size, previous bond or relationship with the teacher, a heterogeneous academic mix of students and the positive social make-up of the class. There is an attempt made to match all these criteria with the needs of the individual child.

Parents have a very important perspective of their child's needs. They may want to share specific information regarding the child's progress and placement with the classroom teacher. At this point a parent may wish to leave the decision to the school now that all the information has been shared. Some parents may choose to insist on a specific placement because of strongly held feelings or because of feelings being strongly expressed by their child. It is important to discuss the concerns with the school and try to reach a solution that is in the best interests of the child. Be careful not to respond to a child's desire to be in a class only because of a like or dislike of another child or teacher. We all know children can be angry at each other one day and friends the next. Also, remember that it is natural for students to experience some anxiety about their new class. Most adjust very quickly.

It is important to work with the school if you have concerns about class placement. Be aware of the message you are giving your child if you and the school have difficulty resolving the concern. The decision should be based on what is best academically, socially and emotionally for the child. Weighing the merits of each factor will help when placing the child in the appropriate class.

Field Trips:
Necessity
or Nicety

Most of what we learn during our lifetime takes place outside the classroom. Clearly it is important that students, particularly as they grow older, see a connection between knowledge gained at school and the so-called real world. Field trips are one strategy schools use to make this connection. Field trips can vary from half-day to several days in length. The nature of the trip, the academic purpose and the location being visited generally determine the length and the cost. Very few educational experiences are available at no cost though field trips arranged by schools generally cost less per person than what individuals or families could arrange. With the economic times as they are and the need for scrutiny schools are attempting to reduce the number of field trips and ensure that valuable learning experiences are associated with each trip.

Field trips are generally used by teachers as an initiating or culminating activity for a particular unit of study. Starting the unit with a field trip serves to motivate the students and allows them to see the whole before the study of the component parts. They see the big picture and start the unit off with a bang. Completing the unit with a field trip allows the students to see in practical terms what they have been studying. Often, depending on the nature of the trip students can apply what they have learned in class to a "real world" situation.

Field trips that involve overnight stays can serve the same purposes outlined above. In most cases these types of excursions involve the graduating class or another group of students studying a very specific topic.

The overnight trip includes a very significant social component. Important social and personal skills are needed to have a successful extended trip with a large group of students and adult chaperones. Students must get along with many others for the entire trip, eating, sleeping and being together for twenty-four hours a day. In many cases this trip may be the first occasion the students have been away from the comforts and security of home and parents. Students must look after their own personal hygiene, tidy their rooms, be on time for meals and the bus, organize themselves so they have the necessary material and appropriate clothing and manage their spending money. Finally they are also expected to behave in a positive manner at all times, co-operate with others and be positive ambassadors for their school. This is no easy task, particularly if we look at the daily interaction we may have with our own children. Regardless of these significant expectations most students will have fond memories of their overnight field trip. Their memories of this trip will stay with them far longer than the subject of any one specific classroom lesson during that school

year. Most of us still remember our trips to Expo 67, Quebec City or Ottawa and we will for years to come.

Although overnight trips generally take place in the spring term schools are taking extended trips earlier in the year. One very positive result of a trip is the bonding and good working relationship that develops between the students and their teachers. If this relationship building were to occur earlier in the school year the effect on student achievement and positive working environment in the classroom could be very beneficial.

Our first experience in any situation is often our most memorable. If the extended trip happens to be a personal first for any of the students the impact can also be very significant, long lasting and meaningful. The purpose should be to extend learning, provide experiences that cannot be duplicated in class (seeing a whale on the east coast, or standing on the Plains of Abraham) and motivate for future learning. Extended or single day trips, if chosen wisely, with thorough organization, direction and purpose, can provide excellent learning experiences for students.

"No More Victims: No More Victimizers"

As society changes so does the role of our schools. As we read the media accounts over the last number of years we are made increasingly aware of the growing incidence of violence in our community. Often, the situations in the larger communities we read about or see on the six-o'clock news serve to make us aware of but may not always reflect our particular situation. We need to look specifically at our particular school and community for accurate information.

Schools, whether as a result of a perceived need or an attempt to be pro-active, have adopted anti-violence curriculum materials in their programs. The general aim of many of these programs is to teach children the social skills necessary to deal with people and problem situations in a positive manner. It is expected that positive spinoffs would include less aggressive behaviour, enhanced problem solving abilities and more focussed attention in class. A growing number of schools are now determining whether they need this type of program.

One anti-violence curriculum now being used by an increasing number of schools is called *Second Step*. This curriculum was developed by the Committee for Children in Seattle, Washington. The *Second Step* program aims to reduce the number of victims and victimizers by reducing impulsive and aggressive behaviour in children and increasing their level of social competence.

To be effective, the program must be taught by the classroom teacher. The classroom teacher is a very significant person in the life of the student and so is best suited to deliver the program. Lessons involve discussion of various scenarios between children of comparable age. Role playing and other individual and group activities round out the program. An important element in the program is the transfer of training. The concept here is that the teacher and other knowledgeable school staff will relate the topics of the lessons to other situations that occur during school time. Parents are also involved through informal discussions and letters of information about the specific topics covered in class and how they can support the program at home. This is only one of a number of positive initiatives taking place in our schools.

If schools, working in concert with parents and community agencies, can teach our students strategies to control anger and impulsive behaviour, and increase empathy for others, our children and society will be far better off. We will truly progress toward a community with "no more victims and no more victimizers".

Committee For Children, *Second Step: Youth Violence Prevention Curriculum*. Seattle, Washington, USA. 1993.

We all know the joys of long car trips with young children.

Holiday Homework

Despite the difficult economic times many families continue to take an annual vacation. The vacation may take place during scheduled school breaks or when school is in session. Parents, concerned that their children will miss out on specific information, often ask the teacher for homework to be completed while away. The type and amount of work will depend on a number of different factors. When deciding with the teacher what work is appropriate, you may want to consider the following:

1. A great deal of learning takes place beyond the classroom. The vacation you take will expose your child to a different culture. This is an excellent opportunity to develop vocabulary and increase knowledge and understanding.

All the experiences children have enhance their knowledge and they draw upon this during future reading and writing activities.

2. Use the holiday as an opportunity for relaxation. Enhance your relationships by enjoying activities together. Any homework should be approached as a

positive activity. If it becomes tedious and creates tension, its value becomes questionable. You will need to decide what and how much work is possible or appropriate.

3. In some subject areas it may be difficult for the teacher to suggest homework because specific teaching and class work is necessary. The teacher may suggest alternate learning activities based on what is possible.

4. Holidays that extend for two weeks or more may require that your child take some work to keep pace with the knowledge and skills the class will develop.

Long term writing and research assignments may also be appropriate work. If the work relates somehow to the location you are visiting this should help your child see the relevance of holiday homework. The assignment may require you to do some teaching before your child can proceed. You may also find that a concerted effort to catch up may be required when you return. This is one drawback to taking children out of school before a regular school break.

The following ideas may be useful for holidays:
a. Bring or purchase some reading material for your children. Novels, magazines, newspapers of subject related materials are all useful.
b. Have your children keep a journal or diary of the places they visit, and the things they see and learn.

c. A powerful strategy to further the value of the journal involves giving your children a camera and allowing them to take pictures of important events. These pictures can be included in the journal to provide a lasting record of the trip. The photographs may involve plants, animals, buildings or events seen during the trip. They could also take the form of personal firsts. The first time your child swims in salt water, sees a palm tree, visits Disney World or flies in a plane could all be subjects for the journal and the camera. Of course you will have to modify the journal activity for younger children. Regardless, your child will be left with valuable learning experiences and a lasting record of many personal firsts.

Above all else, remember the purpose of your vacation and try to find an appropriate balance between leisure and work.

Surviving Long Car Trips

You may be thinking of packing the family into the car and heading across town or across the country for some relaxation. Unfortunately the relaxing part will not begin until you get to your destination. Children need attention, space and diversions to keep their energy level from overwhelming their parents. An enclosed space, like a car, does not allow for this and we can all imagine the results. If cancelling the trip is not an option there are a number of things you can try that should make the driving portion more comfortable and productive for the children and you. Here are five suggestions for surviving car trips with your sanity intact:

1. Children need to know what behaviour you expect and what is inappropriate. Tell them in a positive but assertive way what you expect. Tell them what you are going to do to assure this and have them make suggestions about the role they can play.

2. You may wish to sweeten the pot if you feel it is appropriate. Make a reward that you and the children chose jointly, contingent on their behaviour while on route. This approach basically says "if you do this, then I'll do that." It is also more effective if the time involved

is of reasonable length. It is unreasonable to expect children to behave as you would wish in all situations for days at a time. For brief periods, where they perceive a positive outcome possible, good behaviour should follow.

3. Have your children bring along games that they could play individually or with someone else. Some suggestions might include toy figures or card games. The fewer the pieces the better. Games with magnetic pieces are also good.

4. Bring along some educational material. Individually, or with the children, decide on which story books, picture books and colouring books they would like. Taped music and stories are also great if you have a cassette player available. Portable video games are very effective for calming children, unless of course you have just one game and two or three children. Regardless of your feelings about them portable video games focus children's attention with a sedative effect. Remember, you should control the games. Bring them out one at a time as required otherwise children may have too many options and not concentrate on anything.

5. There are many verbal games and activities that you can try. Although all are done for fun many have a significant educational value in the area of language and mathematics. Most require no preparation but they will keep the kids occupied and having fun.

i.   Make your oldest child the navigator. Give this child a map and have him or her read road signs and update everyone on your progress.

ii.   Play the Counting Game. Have the children count things such as the number of trucks, cars like yours, buses, Christmas lights, etc.

iii.   Play a trivia/ Carmen Sandiago type of question-and-answer game. Kids love being asked questions and giving answers.

iv.   Play a game I call "Tennis/Elbow/Foot". This is a rhyming and word association game for older children. Play with any number of people. Each person goes in turn and gives a word that either rhymes with or is somehow associated with the word given by the previous person. You have five seconds to answer. Answer incorrectly and you are out. To start the game the first person simply chooses a word. Great fun but it can be difficult!

v.   Play rhyming words. You give the children a word and they think of all the words that rhyme with it. This is one strategy to improve spelling.

vi.   Play *What's My Rule?* This is a classification game. Everyone takes a turn. To begin, choose three or four related words then the other players tell you the rule you used to classify them. Classification is one of the basic thinking skills.

vii.   Play *I Spy*. This is an old standard that asks the players to observe carefully.

viii.   Tell or read some jokes or riddles. Everyone loves a good joke.

ix. Sing some of the children's favourite songs.

x. If you know the major sights or landmarks you will be passing give your children a list of clues you have prepared ahead of time. Alert them when you are getting close. This way they are engaged actively in observation throughout the trip.

You probably have many other activities to add to the list. The more variety throughout the trip the better. If something is working, go with it. Conversely if you find some activity is ineffective, drop it. All the problems associated with long car trips may not disappear but with good planning and some variety you should be able to make your trip more comfortable and pleasant, for all the family. If all else fails, consider flying next time!

No T.V. Days

Although television can be used as an effective learning tool, it also has the potential to be one of the best sedatives for children. Many parents willingly turn on the television to get some relief from the children when indoor play develops to teasing, badgering, not sharing and constantly being at mom or dad. If the situation is such that mom and dad can give the children more attention they may start to play nicely again. Otherwise, the television alternative is an easy solution to the problem of attention seeking.

School breaks are usually the times when television may be relied on too much to occupy the children. If there is more than one child in the family each child probably has preferred shows. One strategy to limit T.V. watching is to allow the children to choose one or two shows each day and spend only that time in front of the T.V. It becomes difficult to ensure that each child will watch only shows they chose if younger or older siblings are also watching at different times. The T.V. could conceivably be on for hours. The children are asked to decide which shows they will watch with the intent being to reduce the amount of time watching T.V. In fact the opposite may occur.

Starting Small: Thinking Big

The idea of a "No T.V. Day" may sound like an impossibility for some kids to cope with. However this is one way that the amount of T.V. watching can be monitored and reduced. Whether on alternate days or once or twice a week, children may find it difficult but it will cause them to think harder and be more creative about how to spend their time.

Children come to rely heavily on television and identify closely with the characters. Children may even become grumpy or suffer withdrawl symptoms when television is restricted. Parents need to understand this and help their children with suggestions for play on "No T.V. Days".

PRINTED BY
IMPRIMERIE D'ÉDITION MARQUIS
IN FEBRUARY 1995
MONTMAGNY (QUÉBEC)